CW01431778

Flipper Zero: your cyber dolphin hacker.

All you need to know

The most **comprehensive** and **practical** guide for novices and experienced enthusiasts to discover how to use the multifunctional device to explore and interact with the digital world with all its **secrets**.

If you do not yet know what flipper zero is or its features and uses this book is for you.

Welcome to the book that will introduce you to the world of hacking with Flipper Zero, the multifunction device that will allow you to communicate and interact with the digital world in ways you never imagined. This book is written by a hacking enthusiast who has spent years researching, experimenting, and sharing techniques, tricks, and tips for making the best use of this tool. The author is not only an expert in hacking, but also an advocate of the ethical developments of this discipline, which aims to explore, understand and improve the world around us without harming or violating the privacy of others. The author will guide you step-by-step through the use of Flipper Zero, explaining its features, advantages and limitations. You will learn how to read, clone and emulate RFID tags, radio controls, access keys and more. You will also generate custom radio signals, manually setting the frequency, modulation, power and data to be transmitted. And that's not all: Flipper Zero is also your cyber-dolphin, a friendly virtual animal that accompanies you on your adventures and helps you discover the secrets hidden around you. This book will show you how to have fun with your cyber-dolphin, how to customize it, and how to make it interact with other Flipper Zeroes. This book is designed for all hacking enthusiasts, both beginners and experts. It doesn't matter if you already have experience with other devices or if you are a novice: you are sure to find something interesting and useful in these pages. The book is divided into thematic chapters, which you can follow in order or skip depending on your interests and needs. Each chapter contains theoretical explanations, practical examples, and Python codes for more advanced signal generation. The book also contains appendices with additional information, such as technical specifications of Flipper Zero, sources for further study, and useful links. We hope you enjoy this book and find it helpful in your hacking journey with Flipper Zero. Happy reading and happy hacking!

INDEX

- Chapter 3: Practical Applications of Flipper Zero
  1. How to test the security of your digital systems with Flipper Zero
  2. How to clone and simulate access cards, remote controls, electronic keys and other devices
  3. Practical uses of Flipper Zero to clone and simulate devices
  4. How to create your own custom applications with Flipper Zero
  5. How to interact with other Flipper Zero users via the dolphin network
  6. How to have fun with Flipper Zero: games, challenges, Easter eggs and more
- Conclusion
  - Why Flipper Zero is a unique and innovative device
  - What are the benefits and risks of using Flipper Zero
  - What are the future prospects for Flipper Zero
  - Where to find more information and resources on Flipper Zero

INTRODUCTION

Flipper Zero is a multifunctional handheld device that allows you to explore and interact with the digital world around you. Whether you are an avid hacker, a cybersecurity professional, or just curious, Flipper Zero gives you a range of tools and features to discover, analyze, and manipulate various digital systems such as radio protocols, access control systems, RFID, NFC, and infrared. Flipper Zero is completely open source and customizable, so you can extend it in any way you like. In addition, Flipper Zero has a soul: the virtual dolphin that lives inside it. The dolphin is your cybernautical friend who accompanies you on your digital adventures, helps you use the device, and reacts to what you do. The dolphin also has its own personality and needs, so you will have to take care of it and feed it with the data you find.

In this book, we will guide you through the discovery of Flipper Zero, its origins and history, its basic and advanced features, its practical applications, and its future prospects. We will show you how to use Flipper Zero to test the security of your digital systems, clone and simulate access cards, remote controls, electronic keys, and other devices, create your own custom applications with Flipper Zero, interact with other Flipper Zero users via the Dolphin Network, and have fun with Flipper Zero with games, challenges, Easter eggs, and more. We'll also give you tips and advice on how to use Flipper Zero responsibly and ethically, avoiding causing harm or breaking the law.

If you're ready to dive into the world of Flipper
Zero, then let's get started!

Chapter 1:
The basic functionality of Flipper Zero

In this chapter, we will teach you how to use the basic functionality of your Flipper Zero, the multifunctional portable device for hacking, pentesting, and cybersecurity enthusiasts. We'll show you how to turn the device on and off, how to navigate the menu and select options, how to update firmware and install new applications, how to connect Flipper Zero to your computer or smartphone, and how to use the USB port, microSD reader, and GPIO pins. Follow us step by step and discover everything you can do with your Flipper Zero.

1.1 HOW TO TURN THE DEVICE ON AND OFF

To turn on your Flipper Zero, you must long press the **OK** button located in the center of the directional pad. You will see an animated logo appear on the LCD screen with a dolphin jumping out of the water. This is your cybernautical friend who lives inside your Flipper Zero. The dolphin has its own personality and needs, so you will have to take care of it and feed it with the data you find. The dolphin will also help you use the device and react to what you do. I will tell you more about the dolphin in the next chapter.

To turn off your Flipper Zero, you must long press the **BACK** button located next to the directional pad. You will see a message appear on the LCD screen asking you to confirm your choice. You can select Yes or No using the **LEFT** and **RIGHT buttons**, and confirm with the **OK** button. If you choose Yes, your Flipper Zero will turn off and you will see an animated logo with a dolphin diving underwater on the LCD screen. If you choose No, your Flipper Zero will return to the main menu.

1.2 HOW TO NAVIGATE THE MENU AND SELECT OPTIONS

The main menu of your Flipper Zero consists of a series of icons representing the different applications and features available. You can scroll through the icons using the **UP** and **DOWN** buttons on the directional pad. The selected icon will be highlighted by a white frame. To open the application or feature corresponding to the selected icon, you must press the **OK** button. To return to the main menu from any application or feature, you must press the **BACK** button.

Some applications or features have submenus with additional options. You can access the submenus by pressing the **OK** button when you are on the icon of the main application or feature. You can scroll through the options in the submenus by using the **UP** and **DOWN** buttons on the directional pad. To select the desired option, you must press the **OK** button. To return to the previous menu, you must press the **BACK** button.

1.3 HOW TO UPGRADE FIRMWARE AND INSTALL NEW APPLICATIONS

Firmware is the software that controls the basic functions of your Flipper Zero. The firmware is updated periodically by the developers to improve performance, correct errors, and add new features. To update your Flipper Zero's firmware, you must follow these steps:

Connect your Flipper Zero to your computer via a USB cable.
Download the latest firmware version from the official Flipper Zero website.
Copy the firmware file into the FLIPPER/FIRMWARE folder of your Flipper Zero.
Disconnect your Flipper Zero from the computer.
Turn on your Flipper Zero and go to the Settings menu.
Select the Update Firmware option and press the **OK** button.
Follow the instructions on the LCD screen and wait for the update process to complete.
To install new applications on your Flipper Zero, you must follow these steps:

Connect your Flipper Zero to your computer via a USB cable.
Download the applications you want to install from the official Flipper Zero website or other reliable sources.

Copy the application files to the FLIPPER/APPS folder on your Flipper Zero.

Disconnect your Flipper Zero from the computer.

Turn on your Flipper Zero and go to the Applications menu.

Select the application you want to start and press the **OK** button.

1.4 HOW TO CONNECT FLIPPER ZERO TO YOUR COMPUTER OR SMARTPHONE

You can connect your Flipper Zero to your computer or smartphone via a USB cable or via Bluetooth. This allows you to transfer data, files, and applications between devices, and control your Flipper Zero remotely.

To connect your Flipper Zero to your computer or smartphone via a USB cable, you need to follow these steps:

Connect your Flipper Zero to your computer or smartphone via a USB cable.
Turn on your Flipper Zero and go to the Settings menu.
Select the USB Mode option and press the **OK** button.
Choose the mode you prefer from the following:
Mass Storage: your Flipper Zero will function as a USB flash drive, allowing you to access the internal memory and microSD card.
Serial Port: Your Flipper Zero will function as a virtual serial port, allowing you to communicate with the device via a terminal or a dedicated program.
HID Keyboard: your Flipper Zero will function as a virtual keyboard, allowing you to send commands to your computer or smartphone via the device's buttons.
HID Mouse: Your Flipper Zero will function as a virtual mouse,

allowing you to control the cursor on your computer or smartphone via the device's buttons.

To connect your Flipper Zero to your computer or smartphone via Bluetooth, you need to follow these steps:

Turn on Bluetooth on your computer or smartphone.
Turn on your Flipper Zero and go to the Settings menu.
Select the Bluetooth option and press the **OK** button.
Choose the Enable Bluetooth option and press the **OK** button.
Choose the option Make visible and press the **OK** button.
On your computer or smartphone, search for available Bluetooth devices and select the one called FLIPPER-ZERO-XXXX, where XXXX is the last four digits of your device's serial number.
Enter PIN code 0000 to pair the devices.
On your computer or smartphone, start the Flipper Connect app or another Flipper Zero compatible app.
Follow the app's instructions to establish the connection and control your Flipper Zero remotely.

1.5 HOW TO USE THE USB PORT, MICROSD READER AND GPIO PINS

The USB port on your Flipper Zero is located on the right side of the device. You can use the USB port to connect your Flipper Zero to your computer or smartphone, as we saw in the previous section. You can also use the USB port to power your Flipper Zero via a power outlet, an external battery, or a solar panel. In addition, you can use the USB port to connect external accessories that are compatible with Flipper Zero, such as a webcam, printer, Wi-Fi stick, or GPS2 module.

Your Flipper Zero's microSD reader is located on the left side of the device. You can use the microSD reader to insert a memory card to expand the storage capacity of your Flipper Zero. You can use the microSD card to save data, files, and applications that do not fit in the device's internal memory. You can also use the microSD card to transfer data and files between your Flipper Zero and other devices, such as your computer or smartphone. To insert or remove the microSD card, you must gently push the card into the reader until you hear a click.

1.6 GPIO WITH FLIPPER ZERO

GPIO stands for General Purpose Input/Output. These are electrical pins found on the bottom edge of Flipper Zero that allow you to connect sensors or additional components to expand the functionality of the device. In this chapter, we will see how to use the GPIO pins to communicate with external devices, how to configure the pins as inputs or outputs, how to read or write digital or analog values, and how to use protocols such as I2C, SPI, or UART.

Pinout

Flipper Zero has 10 GPIO pins, numbered 0 to 9, located on the bottom edge of the device. Each pin has a specific function, which can be changed through software. The following table summarizes the functions of the GPIO pins:

Pin	Function	Description
0	TX	Serial Transmitter (UART)
1	RX	Serial receiver (UART)
2	SDA	I2C data
3	SCL	Clock I2C
4	ADC	Analog-to-digital converter
5	DAC	Digital-to-analog converter
6	PWM	Pulse width modulation

7	CS	Chip select (SPI)
8	MOSI	Master out slave in (SPI)
9	MISO	Master in slave out (SPI)

To connect an external device to the GPIO pins, a jumper cable or a breadboard can be used. Care should be taken not to connect devices that require a voltage higher than 3.3 V, otherwise you may damage the device. Also, care should be taken not to create short circuits or incorrect connections.

Configuration

To configure GPIO pins, one can use the "Tools" > "GPIO" menu on the device, or write a script in Python or C. The "Tools" > "GPIO" menu allows you to select a pin and set its mode (input or output), its value (high or low), and its type (digital or analog). In addition, the menu shows the status of the pins in real time.

To write a script in Python or C, you can use the built-in editor on the device, or use an external editor on your computer and transfer the script via USB or Bluetooth. The script must have the extension ".py" or ".c" and must be saved in the "scripts" or "c" folder in the root of the internal memory or microSD card. To run the script, simply select it from the "Tools" > "Scripts" or "Tools" > "C" menu.

To interact with GPIO pins via script, one can use the "flipper" module in Python or the "flipper.h" library in C, which offer different classes and functions to configure, read and write pin values. More details on the documentation of the "flipper" module or the "flipper.h" library can be found on the official website.

Example of a Python script that configures pin 4 as an analog input and shows the value on the display:

```
# Import the flipper module
import flipper

# Create a GPIO object
gpio = flipper.GPIO()

# Create an LCD object
lcd = flipper.LCD()

# Configures pin 4 as an analog input.
```

```
gpio.set_mode(4, gpio.INPUT)
gpio.set_type(4, gpio.ANALOG)

# Infinite loop
while True:
  # Reads the analog value of pin 4
  value = gpio.read(4)

  # Cleans the display
  lcd.clear()

  # Writes the value on the display
  lcd.print("Analog value: %d" % value)

  # Wait a tenth of a second
  flipper.sleep(0.1)
```

Communication

GPIO pins allow communication with external devices using different protocols, such as I2C, SPI, or UART. These protocols are serial communication standards that use electrical signals to transmit and receive data. Each protocol has specific characteristics, such as the number of pins required, the type of connection (synchronous or asynchronous), the role of the devices (master or slave), and the data format.

I2C stands for Inter-Integrated Circuit. It is a synchronous protocol that uses two pins, SDA (data) and SCL (clock), to create a bidirectional connection between a master device and one or more slave devices. The master is the device that initiates and controls the communication, while the slaves are the devices that respond to the master's requests. Each device has a unique address that identifies it on the line. The master can read or write data to or from a slave by specifying its address and the direction of transmission. Data are transmitted in 8-bit packets, followed by an ack (acknowledgment) bit indicating whether the transmission was successful.

SPI stands for Serial Peripheral Interface. It is a synchronous protocol that uses four pins, CS (chip select), MOSI (master out slave in), MISO (master in slave out) and SCK (serial clock), to create a full-duplex connection between a master device and one or more slave devices. The master is the device that generates the clock signal and selects the slave to communicate with via the CS pin. The master and slave exchange data simultaneously via the MOSI and MISO pins. Data are transmitted in 8-bit packets, aligned with the rising or falling edge of the clock signal.

UART stands for Universal Asynchronous Receiver-Transmitter. It is an asynchronous protocol that uses two pins, TX (transmitter) and RX (receiver), to create a half-duplex connection between two devices. The two devices must have the same baud rate and data format (number of bits, parity bits, stop bits). Data are transmitted in packets of 8 bits, preceded by a start bit and followed by a stop bit.

To use these protocols with GPIO pins, one can use the "Tools" > "GPIO" menu on the device, or write a script in Python or C. The "Tools" > "GPIO" menu allows you to select a protocol and set the parameters needed for communication, such as address, direction, baud rate, data format, etc. In addition, the menu allows you to send or receive data via GPIO pins.

To write a script in Python or C, you can use the built-in editor on the device, or use an external editor on your computer and transfer the script via USB or Bluetooth. The script must have the extension ".py" or ".c" and must be saved in the "scripts" or "c" folder in the root of the internal memory or microSD card. To run the script, simply select it from the "Tools" > "Scripts" or "Tools" > "C" menu.

To interact with the protocols via the script, one can use the "flipper" module in Python or the "flipper.h" library in C, which offer different classes and functions to configure, send and receive data via GPIO pins. More details on the documentation of the "flipper" module or the "flipper.h" library can be found on the official website.

Example of a Python script that uses the I2C protocol to communicate with a DHT22 temperature and humidity sensor:

```python
# Import the flipper module
import flipper

# Import the time module to manage time
import time

# Defines the I2C address of the DHT22 sensor (0x5C).
DHT22_ADDR = 0x5C

# Defines the I2C command to read data from the DHT22 sensor (0xAC)
DHT22_CMD = 0xAC

# Create an I2C object
i2c = flipper.I2C()

# Create an LCD object
lcd = flipper.LCD()

# Infinite loop
while True:
    # Send I2C command to DHT22 sensor to request data
    i2c.write(DHT22_ADDR, [DHT22_CMD])

    # Wait 50 milliseconds for the sensor to process the request
    time.sleep(0.05)

    # Reads 4 bytes of data from the DHT22 sensor.
    data = i2c.read(DHT22_ADDR, 4)

    # If the data is valid
    if data:
        # Extracts temperature and humidity values from the data.
```

```
humidity = data[0] + data[1] / 10.0
temperature = data[2] + data[3] / 10.0

# Cleans the display
lcd.clear()

# Writes temperature and humidity values to the display
lcd.print("Temperature: %.1f C\nUmidity: %.1f %%" % (temperature,
humidity))

 # Wait a second
 flipper.sleep(1)
```

The first chapter comes to an end. I hope you enjoyed it and found it useful. In the next chapter, I will tell you about the advanced features of Flipper Zero, such as intercepting and emulating RFID and NFC tags, communicating with IoT devices and access control systems via radio frequency, sending and receiving infrared signals, and using the Touch Memory module and Bluetooth. Don't miss it!

CHAPTER 2:

The advanced features of Flipper Zero

In this chapter, we will teach you how to use the advanced features of your Flipper Zero, the multifunctional handheld device for hacking, pentesting, and cybersecurity enthusiasts. We'll show you how to intercept and emulate RFID and NFC tags, how to communicate with IoT devices and access control systems via radio frequency, how to send and receive infrared signals, how to use the Touch Memory module to read and write data to ibutton keys, and how to use Bluetooth to connect to other devices or Flippers. Follow us step by step and discover all you can do with your Flipper Zero.

2.1 HOW TO INTERCEPT AND EMULATE RFID AND NFC TAGS

RFID (Radio Frequency Identification) and NFC (Near Field Communication) are two technologies that allow data to be transmitted remotely via radio waves. These technologies are used to identify and exchange information between objects, such as credit cards, passports, badges, tags, and more. Each object equipped with RFID or NFC has a tag that contains a unique code and other data. The tag can be read by a reader that generates a magnetic field and sends a request to the tag. The tag responds to the reader by sending its data.

Your Flipper Zero can function as both a reader and an RFID or NFC tag. You can use your Flipper Zero to intercept data from RFID or NFC tags you find around you, and to emulate the RFID or NFC tags you want to simulate. To do this, you need to follow these steps:

Turn on your Flipper Zero and go to the RFID/NFC menu.
Select the Interceptor option and press the **OK** button.
Move your Flipper Zero closer to the RFID or NFC tag you want to intercept.
Wait for your Flipper Zero to detect the tag and show you its data on the LCD screen.

You can save the tag data in the memory of your Flipper Zero by pressing the **OK** button.

You can scroll through the tag data using the **UP** and **DOWN** buttons on the directional pad.

You can return to the RFID/NFC menu by pressing the **BACK** button.

To emulate an RFID or NFC tag with your Flipper Zero, you need to follow these steps:

Turn on your Flipper Zero and go to the RFID/NFC menu.

Select the Emulator option and press the **OK** button.

Choose the type of tag you want to emulate from those available. You can use the **UP** and **DOWN** buttons on the directional pad to scroll through the options, and the **OK** button to select them.

Enter the data you want to associate with the tag you are emulating. You can use the **LEFT** and **RIGHT** buttons on the directional pad to move between fields, and the **UP** and **DOWN** buttons to change values. You can also use data from a previously intercepted tag by pressing the **BACK** button.

Confirm the data of the tag you are emulating by pressing the **OK** button.

Bring your Flipper Zero closer to the RFID or NFC reader you want to fool.

Wait for your Flipper Zero to respond to the reader by sending the data from the tag you are emulating.

You can return to the RFID/NFC menu by pressing the **BACK** button.

Using these features, you can clone and simulate credit cards, passports, badges, tags, and other RFID or NFC-enabled items. This can be useful for testing the security of your systems, or for having fun with your friends. Be careful, though, not to violate the law or the privacy of others, and not to cause harm or inconvenience to yourself or others.

2.2 HOW TO COMMUNICATE WITH IOT DEVICES AND ACCESS CONTROL SYSTEMS VIA RADIO FREQUENCY

IoT (Internet of Things) is the term for the set of Internet-connected objects that can communicate with each other and with other devices. Some examples of IoT objects are smart light bulbs, thermostats, cameras, speakers, sensors and more. Access control systems, on the other hand, are systems that regulate access to certain areas or resources through authentication mechanisms. Some examples of access control systems are electronic locks, turnstiles, barriers, gates, and more.

Many IoT objects and access control systems use radio frequency to communicate with each other or with other devices . Radio frequency is the spectrum of electromagnetic waves that propagate through the air and can carry information. Radio frequency has several bands, each with a different frequency and wavelength. Some bands are used for specific purposes, such as the FM band for radio, the GSM band for mobile telephony, the Wi-Fi band for wireless networks, and so on.

Your Flipper Zero can communicate with IoT devices and access control systems via radio frequency. You can use your Flipper Zero to send and receive radio signals on different bands, and to change the parameters of the signals, such as frequency, modulation, coding, and more. To do this, you need to follow these steps:

Turn on your Flipper Zero and go to the Radio menu.
Select the Transceiver option and press the **OK** button.
Choose the band you want to use from those available. You can use the **UP** and **DOWN** buttons on the directional pad to scroll through the options, and the **OK** button to select them.
Set the parameters of the radio signal you want to send or receive. You can use the **LEFT** and **RIGHT** buttons on the directional pad to move between parameters, and the **UP** and **DOWN** buttons to change them. You can also use the parameters of a previously intercepted radio signal by pressing the **BACK** button.
To send a radio signal, press the **OK** button. Your Flipper Zero will transmit the radio signal set on the LCD screen.
To receive a radio signal, press the **BACK** button. Your Flipper Zero will enter receive mode and show you the detected radio signal on the LCD screen.
You can return to the Radio menu by pressing the **BACK** button.
Using these capabilities, you can communicate with IoT devices and access control systems via radio frequency. This can be useful for controlling smart light bulbs, thermostats, cameras, speakers, sensors, and more. You can also open electronic locks, turnstiles, barriers, gates, and more. Be careful, though, not to interfere with others' communications or essential services, and not to violate the law or others' privacy.

2.3 HOW TO SEND AND RECEIVE INFRARED SIGNALS

Infrared is an electromagnetic wave that has a wavelength longer than visible light but shorter than radio waves. Infrared is used to transmit data at a distance via beams invisible to the human eye. This technology is used to control various electronic devices, such as televisions, air conditioners, DVD players, and more. Each electronic device has an infrared receiver that can detect infrared signals sent by a remote control. Each remote control has an infrared transmitter that can send infrared signals encoded according to the button pressed.

Your Flipper Zero can function as both a remote control and an infrared receiver. You can use your Flipper Zero to send and receive infrared signals encoded according to different protocols. To do this, you need to follow these steps:

Turn on your Flipper Zero and go to the Infrared menu.
Select the Transmitter option and press the **OK** button.
Choose the protocol you want to use from those available. You can use the **UP** and **DOWN** buttons on the directional pad to scroll through the options, and the **OK** button to select them.
Choose the command you want to send from those available. You can use the **UP** and **DOWN** buttons on the directional pad to scroll through the options, and the **OK** button to select them.
Pointing your Flipper Zero at the electronic device you want to control, press the **OK** button. Your Flipper Zero will send the

infrared signal corresponding to the chosen command.

You can return to the Infrared menu by pressing the **BACK** button.

To receive an infrared signal with your Flipper Zero, you must follow these steps:

Turn on your Flipper Zero and go to the Infrared menu.

Select the Receiver option and press the **OK** button.

Pointing the remote control at your Flipper Zero, press the button you want to intercept.

Wait for your Flipper Zero to detect the infrared signal and show you the protocol and signal code on the LCD screen.

You can save the signal in the memory of your Flipper Zero by pressing the **OK** button.

You can return to the Infrared menu by pressing the **BACK** button.
Using these features, you can control various electronic devices via infrared signals. This can be useful for turning on or off televisions, air conditioners, DVD players, and more. You can also clone existing remotes or create your own custom remotes. Be careful not to disturb other users of electronic devices, though, and not to violate the law or the privacy of others.

2.4 HOW TO USE THE TOUCH MEMORY MODULE TO READ AND WRITE DATA TO IBUTTON KEYS

The Touch Memory module is one of the most interesting features of Flipper Zero, allowing you to interact with ibutton keys, also known as Dallas Touch Memory or contact memory. These are small, coin-shaped electronic keys that contain an EEPROM memory and a unique identifier. ibutton keys are used in various areas, such as access control, temperature monitoring, electronic payment, and asset management. In this chapter, we will see how to use Flipper Zero's Touch Memory module to read and write data to ibutton keys, taking advantage of the 1-Wire protocol.

The 1-Wire protocol is a half-duplex serial protocol that allows low-speed (16.3 kbit/s) communication and powering of devices via a single conductor. The 1-Wire protocol involves two types of devices: master and slave. The master is the device that initiates and controls the communication, while the slaves are the devices that respond to the master's orders. In our case, Flipper Zero acts as the master and the ibutton keys as slaves. Each ibutton key has a unique 64-bit serial code, which is used to identify it on the 1-Wire bus.

To connect an ibutton key to Flipper Zero, simply plug it into the circular connector on the top of the device. The connector has two contacts: a center one (DATA+) and an outer one (GND). The ibutton key has the same arrangement of contacts, so just match them to establish the connection. Once the ibutton key is inserted, Flipper Zero automatically detects its presence and shows the serial code of the key and the associated EEPROM memory type on the LCD. For example, if we insert a DS1990A-F5 key, we will see on the display:

iButton detected
Serial: 01-0000000000
Memory: DS1990A

To read or write the data contained in the EEPROM memory of the ibutton key, we need to access the Touch Memory menu of Flipper Zero by pressing the center button on the D-Pad. The Touch Memory menu gives us several options:

-Read : reads data from the EEPROM memory of the ibutton key and shows it on the LCD in hexadecimal format. If the EEPROM memory is protected by a password, we have to enter it before reading the data.

-Write: writes data into the EEPROM memory of the ibutton key, starting from the specified address. We can enter the data manually using the D-Pad or load it from a microSD card inserted in the slot of Flipper Zero. If the EEPROM memory is password protected, we have to enter it before writing data.

-Copy : copies data from one ibutton key to another, keeping the same serial code. This function is useful for cloning ibutton keys used for access control. To use this function, we must have two circular connectors connected to Flipper Zero via GPIO pins. The first connector is used to connect the original ibutton key, while the second is used to connect the blank ibutton key to be copied.

-Password : Set or change the password to protect the EEPROM memory of the ibutton key. The password must be 8 bytes long and is stored in the same EEPROM memory. If we set a password, we need to remember it in order to access the data in the future.

-Erase: erases all data from the EEPROM memory of the ibutton key, returning it to its initial state. This function does not erase the serial code of the key.

These are the main functions of Flipper Zero's Touch Memory module. With these functions we can read and write data to ibutton keys quickly and easily, taking advantage of the potential of the 1-Wire protocol. In addition, we can use Flipper Zero to emulate an ibutton key by sending the desired serial code and data via the circular connector. This function is useful for testing the security of systems based on ibutton keys. For more information on the 1-Wire protocol and ibutton keys, some websites such as:

-        **Official site of Maxim Integrated**, the manufacturer of ibutton keys and 1-Wire devices.

-        **Official site of Flipper** Zero, where technical specifications, instructions and firmware of Flipper Zero can be found.

-        **Wikipedia**, where general information about the 1-Wire protocol and ibutton keys can be found.

2.5 HOW TO USE BLUETOOTH TO CONNECT TO OTHER DEVICES OR FLIPPERS

Bluetooth is a technology that enables short-range data transmission via radio waves. This technology is used to connect various electronic devices together, such as computers, smartphones, speakers, headsets, mice, keyboards, and more. Bluetooth allows data, files, and information to be exchanged between connected devices, and device functions to be controlled remotely.

Your Flipper Zero has a built-in Bluetooth module that allows you to use Bluetooth to connect to other devices or Flippers. You can use your Flipper Zero to send and receive data, files, and applications via Bluetooth, and to use your Flipper Zero as an input or output device for other devices. To do this, you must follow these steps:

Turn on your Flipper Zero and go to the Bluetooth menu.
Select the Enable Bluetooth option and press the **OK** button.
Choose the Search Devices option and press the **OK** button.
Wait for your Flipper Zero to detect Bluetooth devices near you and show you a list on the LCD screen.
Choose the Bluetooth device you want to connect with and press the **OK** button.

Enter the PIN code required to pair the devices. The PIN code can be 0000, 1234, or another device-specific code. You may also receive a pairing request from another device, in which case you must accept or reject it.

Wait for your Flipper Zero to establish a connection with the other Bluetooth device and show you the name and icon of the device on the LCD screen.

You can exchange data, files and applications with the other device by selecting the Transfer option and pressing the **OK** button. You can choose what to transfer from the available options, such as RFID/NFC data, radio data, infrared data, Python or C applications, images, or others. You can also receive data, files and applications from the other device if it sends you something.

You can use your Flipper Zero as an input or output device for the other device by selecting the Mode option and pressing the **OK** button. You can choose from several available modes, such as HID Keyboard, HID Mouse, Serial Port, or Audio. In this mode, you can use the directional pad buttons and the **OK** and **BACK** buttons on your Flipper Zero to control the other device, or you can use the LCD screen or speaker on your Flipper Zero to view or listen to data from the other device.

You can end the connection with the other device by selecting the Disconnect option and pressing the **OK** button. Your Flipper Zero will disconnect from the other Bluetooth device and return to the Bluetooth menu.

Using these steps, you can use Bluetooth to connect to other devices or Flippers with your Flipper Zero. This can be useful for exchanging data, files, and applications with other devices or Flippers, and for using your Flipper Zero as an input or output device for other devices. Be careful, though, not to connect to unknown or untrusted devices, and not to send or receive sensitive or confidential data via Bluetooth.

2.6 SCRIPTING WITH FLIPPER ZERO

Flipper Zero is not only a gadget, but also a development platform that allows you to create and modify custom scripts to perform various tasks. In this chapter, we will see how to write scripts in Python or C, how to upload them to the device, and how to use them to take full advantage of Flipper Zero's potential.

Python:

Python is a high-level programming language that is easy to learn and use and offers many libraries and modules for interacting with various protocols and devices. Flipper Zero supports Python 3.9 and offers an interactive shell accessible through the "Tools" > "Python" menu. From here, you can run Python commands directly on the device, or write and save Python scripts to the internal memory or microSD card.

To write a Python script, you can use the built-in editor on the device, or use an external editor on your computer and transfer the script via USB or Bluetooth. The script must have the extension ".py" and must be saved in the "scripts" folder in the root of the internal memory or microSD card. To run the script, simply select it from the "Tools" > "Scripts" menu.

To interact with the hardware and software features of Flipper Zero, one can use the "flipper" module, which offers different classes and methods to control the display, LEDs, buzzer, buttons, temperature sensor, RFID reader, infrared transmitter, radio module, and more. More details on the documentation of the "flipper" module can be found on the official website.

Some practical examples of applications that can be created by scripting in Python for Flipper Zero are:

Example of a Python script that reads an RFID tag and shows it on the display:

```python
# Import the flipper module
import flipper

# Create an RFID object
rfid = flipper.RFID()

# Create an LCD object
lcd = flipper.LCD()

# Cleans the display
lcd.clear()

# Writes a message on the display
lcd.print("Approach an RFID tag.")

# Infinite loop
while True:
  # Reads an RFID tag if present
  tag = rfid.read()

  # If the tag is valid
  if tag:
    # Cleans the display
    lcd.clear()

    # Writes the type and ID of the tag on the display.
    lcd.print("Type: %s\nID: %s" % (tag.type, tag.id))

    # Emits a beep
    flipper.buzzer.beep()

    # Wait a second
    flipper.sleep(1)
```

```
# Cleans the display
lcd.clear()

# Writes the initial message
lcd.print("Approach an RFID tag.")
```

> ➢ A digital thermometer that shows the temperature detected by the built-in temperature sensor on the display.

```
# Import the flipper module
import flipper

# Create an LCD object
lcd = flipper.LCD()

# Create a temperature object
temp = flipper.Temperature()

# Infinite loop
while True:
  # Reads the temperature in degrees Celsius
  celsius = temp.read()

  # Converts temperature to degrees Fahrenheit.
  fahrenheit = celsius * 1.8 + 32

  # Cleans the display
  lcd.clear()

  # Writes the temperature on the display in both scales.
  lcd.print("Celsius: %.1f C\nFahrenheit: %.1f F" % (celsius, fahrenheit))

  # Wait a second
  flipper.sleep(1)
```

> ➢ A voice translator that records a voice message via the built-in microphone, sends it to an online translation service, and plays it back via the buzzer in a language

chosen by the user.

```
# Import the flipper module
import flipper

# Import the requests module to make HTTP requests.
import requests

# Import json module to manipulate JSON data.
import json

# Defines the URL of the online translation service (Google Translate API).
TRANSLATE_URL    =    "https://translation.googleapis.com/language/
translate/v2"

# Defines the API key for the online translation service.
TRANSLATE_KEY = "YOUR_API_KEY_HERE"

# Defines the languages available for translation.
LANGUAGES = ["en", "it", "fr", "de", "es", "ru", "zh"]

# Create an LCD object
lcd = flipper.LCD()

# Create a microphone object
mic = flipper.Microphone()

# Create a buzzer object
buzzer = flipper.Buzzer()

# Create a variable for the source language (default: English).
source_lang = "en"

# Create a variable for the target language (default: Italian)
target_lang = "en"

# Cleans the display
lcd.clear()

# Writes a welcome message on the display
lcd.print("Welcome to the voice translator!\Use the buttons to choose
languages.")
```

```python
# Infinite loop
while True:
  # Wait for the user to press a button.
  button = flipper.button.wait()

  # If the user presses the top left button.
  if button == flipper.Button.LEFT_TOP:
    # Change the source language to the next value in the language list.
    source_lang = LANGUAGES[(LANGUAGES.index(source_lang) + 1) % len(LANGUAGES)]

    # Cleans the display
    lcd.clear()

    # Writes the new source language on the display.
    lcd.print("Source language: %s" % source_lang.upper())

    # Emits a beep
    buzzer.beep()

    # Wait half a second
    flipper.sleep(0.5)

  # If the user presses the button in the upper right corner.
  elif button == flipper.Button.RIGHT_TOP:
    # Change the target language to the next value in the language list.
    target_lang = LANGUAGES[(LANGUAGES.index(target_lang) + 1) % len(LANGUAGES)]

    # Cleans the display
    lcd.clear()

    # Writes the new target language on the display.
    lcd.print("Target language: %s" % target_lang.upper())

    # Emits a beep
    buzzer.beep()

    # Wait half a second
    flipper.sleep(0.5)
```

```
# If the user presses the bottom left button.
elif button == flipper.Button.LEFT_BOTTOM:
  # Cleans the display
  lcd.clear()

  # Writes a message on the display
  lcd.print("Record your message\nPremi again to stop.")

  # Emits a long beep
  buzzer.beep(0.5)

  # Start recording audio from the microphone.
  mic.start()

  # Wait for the user to press the bottom left button again.
  flipper.button.wait(flipper.Button.LEFT_BOTTOM)

  # Stop recording audio from the microphone.
  mic.stop()

  # Emits a long beep
  buzzer.beep(0.5)

  # Cleans the display
  lcd.clear()

  # Writes a message on the display
  lcd.print("I am translating your message...")

  # Gets the audio data recorded by the microphone as a base64 string.
  audio_data = mic.get_data().encode("base64")

  # Create parameters for HTTP request to online translation service.
  params = {
    "key": TRANSLATE_KEY,
    "q": audio_data,
    "source": source_lang,
    "target": target_lang,
    }, "format": "text",
    "model": "nmt"
```

```
}

# Makes the HTTP request to the online translation service and gets the
response as a JSON object
response = requests.post(TRANSLATE_URL, params=params).json()

# If the response contains a "date" field.
if "data" in response:
    # Extracts the translated text from the response.
    translated_text = response["data"]["translations"][0]["translatedText"]

    # Cleans the display
    lcd.clear()

    # Writes the translated text on the display
    lcd.print(translated_text)

    # Emits a beep
    buzzer.beep()

    # Wait a second
    flipper.sleep(1)

    # Plays the translated text through the buzzer.
    buzzer.speak(translated_text, target_lang)

# Otherwise, if the response contains an "error" field.
elif "error" in response:
    # Extracts the error message from the response.
    error_message = response["error"]["message"]

    # Cleans the display
    lcd.clear()

    # Writes the error message on the display
    lcd.print("Error: %s" % error_message)

    # Emits a double beep
    buzzer.beep(0.2)
    flipper.sleep(0.2)
    buzzer.beep(0.2)
```

```
# Wait two seconds
flipper.sleep(2)

# Cleans the display
lcd.clear()

# Writes the welcome message on the display
lcd.print("Welcome to the voice translator!\Use the buttons to choose languages.")

  # If the user presses the button in the lower right corner.
  elif button == flipper.Button.RIGHT_BOTTOM:
    # Exits the loop and terminates the script.
    break

# Cleans the display
lcd.clear()

# Writes a greeting message on the display.
lcd.print("Goodbye and thank you for using the voice translator!")
```

C

C is a powerful and flexible low-level programming language that offers direct control over hardware and software resources. Flipper Zero supports C11 and offers an integrated development environment (IDE) accessible through the "Tools" > "C" menu. From here, you can write, compile and execute C code directly on the device.

To write C code, you can use the built-in editor on the device, or use an external editor on your computer and transfer the code via USB or Bluetooth. The code must have the extension ".c" and must be saved in the "c" folder in the root of the internal memory or microSD card. To compile and execute the code, simply select it from the "Tools" > "C" menu.

To interact with the hardware and software features of Flipper Zero, one can use the "flipper.h" library, which offers various functions and facilities to control the display, LEDs, buzzer, buttons, temperature sensor, RFID reader, infrared transmitter, radio module, and more. More details on the documentation of the "flipper.h" library can be found on the official website.

Example of C code that sends an infrared signal to turn on a Samsung TV:

```
// Includes the flipper library
#include <flipper.h>

// Defines the code of the Samsung remote control
#define SAMSUNG_POWER 0xE0E040BF

// Defines the frequency of the infrared signal (38 kHz)
#define IR_FREQ 38000

// Defines the duration of one logical bit (562.5 us)
#define LOGIC_BIT 562

// Defines the duration of a high bit (1687.5 us)
#define HIGH_BIT 1687

// Defines the duration of a low bit (562.5 us)
#define LOW_BIT 562

// Defines the duration of a pause (20 ms)
#define PAUSE 20000

// Main function
int main(void) {
  // Create a variable for the code
  uint32_t code = SAMSUNG_POWER;

  // Create a variable for the current bit
  uint8_t bit;

  // Create a variable for the counter
  uint8_t i;
```

```
// Send infrared signal
ir_send(IR_FREQ, LOGIC_BIT, LOGIC_BIT, PAUSE);

// Loop on the 32 bits of the code
for (i = 0; i < 32; i++) {
  // Extracts the most significant bit
  bit = code >> 31;

  // If the bit is high
  if (bit) {
    // Send a high bit
    ir_send(IR_FREQ, LOGIC_BIT, HIGH_BIT, 0);
  }
  // Otherwise
  else {
    // Send a low bit
    ir_send(IR_FREQ, LOGIC_BIT, LOW_BIT, 0);
  }

  // Moves the code to the left by one bit
  code <<= 1;
}

// Send a final pause
ir_send(IR_FREQ, LOGIC_BIT, LOGIC_BIT, PAUSE);

// Return zero
return 0;
}
```

The second chapter comes to an end. I hope you enjoyed it and found it useful. In the next chapter, I will tell you about the practical applications of Flipper Zero, such as testing the security of your digital systems, creating your own applications with Flipper Zero, interacting with other Flipper Zero users via the Dolphin Network, and having fun with Flipper Zero with games, challenges, Easter eggs, and more. Don't miss out!

CHAPTER 3:

Practical applications of Flipper Zero

In this chapter, we will show you how to use your Flipper Zero for practical, fun, and creative purposes. We'll teach you how to test the security of your digital systems, how to create your own apps with Flipper Zero, how to interact with other Flipper Zero users through the Dolphin Network, and how to have fun with Flipper Zero with games, challenges, Easter eggs, and more. Follow us step by step and discover everything you can do with your Flipper Zero.

3.1 HOW TO TEST THE SECURITY OF YOUR DIGITAL SYSTEMS

One of the main purposes of Flipper Zero is to allow you to test the security of your digital systems. With Flipper Zero, you can simulate various attack and defense scenarios, and discover vulnerabilities and weaknesses in your systems. You can also learn how to prevent and counter cyber attacks, and how to protect your data and privacy.

To test the security of your digital systems with Flipper Zero, you must follow these steps:

Choose the digital system you want to test from those you own or have legitimate access to. It can be a computer, smartphone, wireless network, IoT device, access control system, or other. Choose the type of attack you want to simulate from those that Flipper Zero can perform. It can be an RFID/NFC attack, radio attack, infrared attack, USB attack, or other.
Prepare your Flipper Zero to perform the attack. Set the parameters needed for the type of attack you choose, such as frequency, modulation, coding, protocol, and more. You can also use data from a previous intercept or emulation to facilitate the attack.
Move your Flipper Zero closer to the digital system you want to test. Make sure you have good signal coverage and are not detected by any security systems or people.

Perform the attack with your Zero Flipper. Press the appropriate button to send or receive the signal needed for the attack. Wait for your Flipper Zero to show you the outcome of the attack on the LCD screen.

Analyze the results of the attack with your Zero Flipper. Check whether you were able to gain access to the digital system you wanted to test, or whether you encountered any difficulties or blockages. Also check whether you left any traces or damage on the digital system you tested.

Repeat the attack with your Flipper Zero by changing the parameters or changing the type of attack. Try using different techniques and strategies to test the security of the digital system from different angles. Compare your results with previous results.

Assess the security of the digital system you tested with your Zero Flipper. Determine whether the digital system is secure or vulnerable to cyber attacks. Identify the causes and consequences of any vulnerabilities found. Suggest possible solutions or improvements to increase the security of the digital system.

Using these steps, you can test the security of your digital systems with Flipper Zero. This can be useful for learning how to defend yourself against cyber attacks, and for improving your hacking and pentesting skills. Be careful, though, not to test the security of digital systems that do not belong to you or to which you do not have legitimate access, and not to violate the law or the privacy of others.

3.2 HOW TO CLONE AND SIMULATE ACCESS CARDS, REMOTE CONTROLS, ELECTRONIC KEYS AND OTHER DEVICES.

Flipper Zero is a handheld device that allows you to interact with various digital systems, such as radio protocols, access control systems, hardware, and more. One of its most interesting functions is its ability to clone and simulate access cards, remote controls, electronic keys, and other devices that use RFID or NFC technologies. In this chapter, we will look at how to use Flipper Zero to clone and simulate these devices, taking advantage of its various built-in antennas and modules.

To clone a device, we must first read its data and store it in the internal memory of Flipper Zero. To do this, we need to choose the right module based on the frequency and type of device we want to clone. Flipper Zero supports the following frequencies and device types:

- 125 kHz: This is the frequency used by low-frequency (LF) access cards, such as HID Prox or EM4100. These cards are very simple and have no authentication or encryption mechanisms, so they are easy to clone. To read these cards, we have to use Flipper Zero's 125 kHz RFID module, which is located on the bottom of the device. Just bring Flipper Zero close to the card to be read and press the center button on the D-Pad. If the read is successful, we will see the serial code of the card and the associated memory type on the LCD display. For example, if we read an HID Prox card, we will see on the display:

LF RFID detected
Serial: 0000000000
Memory: HID Prox

- 13.56 MHz: This is the frequency used by high-frequency (HF) access cards, such as Mifare Classic or Mifare Ultralight. These cards are more complex and may have authentication or encryption mechanisms, so they are more difficult to clone. To read these cards, we have to use the Flipper Zero's 13.56 MHz NFC module, which is located on the top of the device. Just bring Flipper Zero close to the card to be read and press the center button on the D-Pad. If the reading is successful, we will see the serial code of the card and the associated memory type on the LCD display. For example, if we read a Mifare Classic 1K card, we will see on the display:

HF RFID detected
Serial: 0000000000
Memory: Mifare Classic 1K

- Sub-1 GHz: This is the frequency used by many wireless devices and access control systems, such as garage door remotes, automatic barriers, IoT sensors, and keyless systems. Flipper Zero has a built-in 433

MHz antenna and a CC1101 chip, making it a powerful transmitter capable of covering up to 50 meters away. To read these devices, we must use Flipper Zero's Sub-1 GHz module, which is located on the side of the device. Simply bring Flipper Zero close to the device to be read and press the center button on the D-Pad. If the reading is successful, we will see on the LCD display the code of the received signal and the type of modulation used. For example, if we read a garage door remote control, we will see on the display:

Sub-1 GHz detected
Signal: 0101010101010101010101
Modulation: OOK

- Infrared: This is the technology used by many electronic devices to communicate remotely, such as remote controls for TVs, air conditioners, DVD players, and more. Flipper Zero has a built-in infrared transmitter and receiver, which allow it to send and receive infrared signals. To read these devices, we have to use Flipper Zero's Infrared module, which is located on the front of the device. Simply point Flipper Zero at the device to be read and press the center button on the D-Pad. If the reading is successful, we will see on the LCD display the code of the received signal and the type of protocol used. For example, if we read a TV remote control, we will see on the display:

Infrared detected
Signal: 0000000000000000
Protocol: NEC

- Touch Memory: This is the technology used by some coin-shaped electronic keys, which contain an EEPROM memory and a unique identifier. These keys are used in various areas, such as access control, temperature monitoring, electronic payment, and asset management. Flipper Zero has a circular connector to connect these keys and communicate with them via the 1-Wire protocol. To read these keys, we have to use Flipper Zero's Touch Memory module, which is located on the top of the device. Simply insert the key into the connector and press the center button on the D-Pad. If the reading is successful, we will see the serial code of the key and the associated memory type on the LCD display. For example, if we read a DS1990A-F5 key, we will see on the display:

Touch Memory detected
Serial: 01-0000000000
Memory: DS1990A

Once we have read the data from the device to be cloned, we can store it in Flipper Zero's internal memory, creating a new virtual card in our digital wallet. To do this, we need to press the right button on the D-Pad and choose the Save option. We can also assign a name to our virtual card to easily recognize it in the future.

To simulate a device, we must first select the corresponding virtual card in our digital wallet. To do this, we need to access the Wallet menu of Flipper Zero by pressing the left button on the D-Pad. Here we can see all the virtual cards we have saved and choose the one we want to simulate. Once the virtual card is selected, we can activate the simulation mode by pressing the right button of the D-Pad and choosing the Emulate option. At this point, Flipper Zero will behave like the original device, sending the stored data to the corresponding frequency or technology.

To clone a device to physical media, we must first select the corresponding virtual card in our digital wallet. Then we need to connect the empty physical media to Flipper Zero via the GPIO pins or the circular connector, depending on the type of media. Finally, we need to activate the write mode by pressing the right button of the D-Pad and choosing the Write option. At this point,

Flipper Zero will write the data stored on the physical media, creating an exact copy of the original device.

These are the main functions of Flipper Zero to clone and simulate access cards, remote controls, electronic keys and other devices. With these functions we can test the security of systems based on these technologies and have fun discovering their secrets. For more information on Flipper Zero and its capabilities, some websites such as:

- **Official site of Flipper** Zero, where technical specifications, instructions and firmware of Flipper Zero can be found.

- **Official site of Lab401**, where you can purchase Flipper Zero compatible devices, such as the Proxmark3 and Chameleon Mini.

- **Official site of RFID Tools**, where you can find other Android apps for interacting with RFID and NFC devices.

- **Walrus official website**, where you can download another Android app

3.3 PRACTICAL USES OF FLIPPER ZERO TO CLONE AND SIMULATE DEVICES

In this part, we will look at some concrete examples of how to use Flipper Zero to clone and simulate devices using RFID, NFC, Sub-1 GHz, Infrared, or Touch Memory technologies. These examples are for educational purposes only and should not be used for illegal or malicious purposes.

Clone and simulate a low frequency (LF) access card.

Suppose we have a low frequency (LF) access card that allows us to enter a building or room. We want to clone this card and simulate its behavior with Flipper Zero, so that we can enter without using the physical card. To do this, we need to follow these steps:

- We bring Flipper Zero closer to the card to be cloned and press the center button on the D-Pad. If the reading is successful, we will see on the LCD display the serial code of the card and the associated memory type. For example, if we read a HID Prox card, we will see on the display:

LF RFID detected

Serial: 0000000000
Memory: HID Prox

- We press the right button of the D-Pad and choose the Save option. We can also name our virtual paper to easily recognize it in the future. For example, we can call it "Building Card."

- We access the Wallet menu of Flipper Zero by pressing the left button of the D-Pad. Here we can see all the virtual cards we have saved and choose the one we want to simulate. In our case, we choose "Building Card."

- We activate the simulation mode by pressing the right button of the D-Pad and choosing the Emulate option. At this point, Flipper Zero will behave like the original card, sending the stored serial code at a frequency of 125 kHz.

- We approach Flipper Zero to the RFID reader in the building or room we want to enter and press the center button on the D-Pad. If the simulation is successful, the RFID reader will recognize Flipper Zero as the original card and allow us to enter.

Clone and simulate a high frequency (HF) access card.

Suppose we have a high frequency (HF) access card that allows us to pay for a service or product. We want to clone this card and simulate its behavior with Flipper Zero, so that we can pay without using the physical card. To do this, we need to follow these steps:

- We bring Flipper Zero closer to the card to be cloned and press the center button on the D-Pad. If the reading is successful, we will see on the LCD display the serial code of the card and the associated memory type. For example, if we read a Mifare

Ultralight C card, we will see on the display:

HF RFID detected
Serial: 0000000000
Memory: Mifare Ultralight C

- We press the right button of the D-Pad and choose the Save option. We can also name our virtual card to easily recognize it in the future. For example, we can call it "Bus Card."
- We access the Wallet menu of Flipper Zero by pressing the left button of the D-Pad. Here we can see all the virtual cards we have saved and choose the one we want to simulate. In our case, we choose "Bus Card."
- We activate the simulation mode by pressing the right button on the D-Pad and choosing the Emulate option. At this point, Flipper Zero will behave like the original card, sending the stored serial code at a frequency of 13.56 MHz.
- We bring Flipper Zero closer to the NFC reader of the bus or service we want to pay for and press the center button on the D-Pad. If the simulation is successful, the NFC reader will recognize Flipper Zero as the original card and allow us to pay.

Clone and simulate a garage door remote control

Suppose we have a garage door remote control that uses a Sub-1 GHz frequency to send a signal to the receiver. We want to clone this remote control and simulate its behavior with Flipper Zero, so that we can open or close the garage door without using the physical remote control. To do this, we need to follow these steps:

- We bring Flipper Zero closer to the remote control to be cloned and press the center button on the D-Pad. If the reading is successful, we will see on the LCD display the code of the received signal and the type of modulation used. For example, if we read a remote control that uses an OOK modulation, we will see on the display:

Sub-1 GHz detected
Signal: 010101010101010101010101
Modulation: OOK

- We press the right button on the D-Pad and choose the Save option. We can also name our virtual remote control to easily recognize it in the future. For example, we can call it "Garage Remote Control."
- We access the Wallet menu of Flipper Zero by pressing the left button of the D-Pad. Here we can see all the virtual remotes we have saved and choose the one we want to simulate. In our case, we choose "Garage Remote Control."
- We activate the simulation mode by pressing the right button on the D-Pad and choosing the Emulate option. At this point, Flipper Zero will behave like the original remote control, sending the stored signal at the Sub-1 GHz frequency.
- We point Flipper Zero at the garage door receiver and press the middle button on the D-Pad. If the simulation is successful, the receiver will receive the signal sent by Flipper Zero and open or close the garage door.

Clone and simulate a TV remote control

Suppose we have a TV remote control that uses infrared technology to send a signal to the receiver. We want to clone this remote control and simulate its behavior with Flipper Zero, so that we can control the TV without using the physical remote control. To do this, we need to follow these steps:

- Point Flipper Zero at the remote control to be cloned and press the center button on the D-Pad. If the reading is successful, we will see on the LCD display the code of the received signal and the type of protocol used. For example, if we read a remote control that uses the NEC protocol, we will see on the display:

Infrared detected
Signal: 0000000000000000
Protocol: NEC

- We press the right button on the D-Pad and choose the Save option. We can also name our virtual remote control to easily recognize it in the future. For example, we can call it "TV Remote Control."
- We access the Wallet menu of Flipper Zero by pressing the left button of the D-Pad. Here we can see all the virtual remotes we have saved and choose the one we want to simulate. In our case, we choose "TV remote control."
- We activate the simulation mode by pressing the right button on the D-Pad and choosing the Emulate option. At this point, Flipper Zero will behave like the original remote control, sending the stored signal via the infrared transmitter.
- We point Flipper Zero at the TV receiver and press the middle button on the D-Pad. If the simulation is successful, the receiver will receive the signal sent by Flipper Zero and perform the corresponding action.

Opening other people's car doors with the Sub-1 GHz module

Flipper Zero's Sub-1 GHz module allows you to transmit and receive low-frequency radio signals, which are used by many wireless devices such as car remotes, automatic gates, alarms, and so on. With Flipper Zero, you can clone these signals and use them to control these devices remotely.

For example, if you want to open the door of someone else's car, you must first capture the signal of the original remote control.

To do this, you have to approach the car and wait for the owner to use the remote control. Then, you have to activate the "sniffer" mode of Flipper Zero and press the "A" button to start recording the signal. You should see a bar indicating the strength of the signal on the display of Flipper Zero. When the bar is full, it means you have captured the signal. Press the "A" button again to stop recording.

Now, you can play the cloned signal to open the car door. To do this, you need to activate the "transmitter" mode of Flipper Zero and press the "B" button to send the signal. You should see a green light on Flipper Zero's display indicating that the signal has been transmitted. If all goes well, the car door will open.

To clone the signal of the original remote control, you must be close enough to the car and the owner. If you are too far away, the signal may be weak or disturbed by other radio signals.

To play the cloned signal, you must be close enough to the car and point Flipper Zero at the car's radio receiver. If you are too far away, the signal may not arrive or may be blocked by obstacles such as walls or trees.

To know whether you have captured or transmitted the signal correctly, you can use Flipper Zero's audible or visual feedback. Flipper Zero emits a sound or vibration when it records or sends a signal. You can also see on Flipper Zero's display the type and frequency of the signal.

Warning: this technique works only with remote controls that use simple fixed or rolling codes. More advanced remote controls use encrypted or dynamic codes that cannot be cloned easily. Change the channels of your neighbors' TVs with the Infrared module

Flipper Zero's Infrared module allows you to transmit and receive infrared signals, which are used by many devices such as remote controls for TVs, DVDs, air conditioners, and so on. With Flipper Zero, you can clone these signals and use them to control these devices remotely.

For example, if you want to change the channels on your neighbors' TV, you must first capture the signal from the original remote control. To do this, you need to get close to the TV and point Flipper Zero at the TV's infrared receiver. Then, you need to turn on Flipper Zero's "sniffer" mode and press the "A" button to start recording the signal. You should see a bar indicating the strength of the signal on Flipper Zero's display. When you press a button on the original remote control, you should see a spike in the bar. Press the "A" button again to stop recording.

Now, you can play the cloned signal to change TV channels. To do this, you need to turn on Flipper Zero's "transmitter" mode and press the "B" button to send the signal. You should see a red light on Flipper Zero's display indicating that the signal has been transmitted. If all goes well, the TV will change channels.

To capture the signal from the original remote control, you must be close enough to the TV and have a direct line of sight between Flipper Zero and the TV's infrared receiver. If you are too far away or there are obstacles between Flipper Zero and the TV, the signal may be weak or absent.

To play the cloned signal, you must be close enough to the TV and have a direct line of sight between Flipper Zero and the TV's infrared receiver. If you are too far away or there are obstacles between Flipper Zero and the TV, the signal may not arrive or may be reflected by surfaces such as glass or mirrors.

To know whether you have captured or transmitted the signal correctly, you can use Flipper Zero's audible or visual feedback. Flipper Zero makes a sound or vibration when it records or sends a signal. You can also see on Flipper Zero's display the type and length of the signal.

Warning: this technique works only if you are close enough to the TV and there are no obstacles between Flipper Zero and the TV's infrared receiver.

Pay less for bus tickets with NFC module

Flipper Zero's NFC module allows you to transmit and receive short-range signals, which are used by many devices such as credit cards, passports, bus tickets, and so on. With Flipper Zero, you can read and write these signals and modify them to your liking.

For example, if you want to pay less for bus tickets, you must first read the signal of your bus card. To do this, you need to bring Flipper Zero closer to your bus card and activate Flipper Zero's "reader" mode. You should see on the display of Flipper Zero the information contained in the card, such as the balance, expiration date, security code, and so on.

Now, you can write the changed signal on your bus card. To do this, you have to activate the "writer" mode of Flipper Zero and choose what information to change. You can increase the balance, extend the expiration date, change the security code, and so on. Then, you need to bring Flipper Zero closer to your bus card and press the "B" button to write the signal. You should see a blue light on Flipper Zero's display indicating that the signal has been written. If all goes well, your bus card will be updated with the new information.

To read the signal from your bus card, you must bring Flipper Zero closer to your bus card until you hear a beep or vibration. If you are too far away from the bus card, the signal may not be detected by Flipper Zero.

To write the modified signal on your bus card, you must bring Flipper Zero closer to your bus card until you hear a beep or vibration. If you are too far away from the bus card, the signal may not be written by Flipper Zero.

To know whether you have read or written the signal correctly, you can use Flipper Zero's audible or visual feedback. Flipper Zero makes a sound or vibration when it reads or writes a signal. You can also see on Flipper Zero's display the information in the card.

Caution: this technique works only with bus cards that use NFC technology and do not have advanced protection systems. The most secure bus cards use encrypted chips or unchanging memories that cannot be easily altered.

Creating fake barcodes with the Touch Memory module

Flipper Zero's Touch Memory module allows you to transmit and receive signals by physical contact, which are used by many devices such as electronic keys, smart locks, RFID tags, and so on. With Flipper Zero, you can clone these signals and use them to fool these devices.

For example, if you want to create fake barcodes, you must first capture the signal of an original barcode. To do this, you need to bring Flipper Zero close to the bar code and activate Flipper Zero's "sniffer" mode. You should see on Flipper Zero's display the number corresponding to the bar code.

Now, you can play the cloned signal to create fake barcodes. To do this, you have to activate the "transmitter" mode of Flipper Zero and choose the number to transmit. You can use the same number or change it to your liking. Then, you need to bring Flipper Zero closer to the bar code reader and press the "B" button to send the signal. You should see a yellow light on Flipper Zero's display indicating that the signal has been transmitted. If all goes well, the bar code reader will recognize the fake bar code.

To capture the signal of an original bar code, you must bring Flipper Zero closer to the bar code until you hear a beep or vibration. If you are too far away from the bar code, the signal may not be detected by Flipper Zero.

To play the cloned signal to create fake barcodes, you need to bring Flipper Zero closer to the barcode reader until you hear a beep or vibration. If you are too far away from the bar code reader, the signal may not be transmitted by Flipper Zero.

To know whether you have captured or transmitted the signal

correctly, you can use Flipper Zero's audible or visual feedback. Flipper Zero emits a sound or vibration when it records or sends a signal. You can also see on Flipper Zero's display the number corresponding to the bar code.

Please note: This technique works only with barcodes that use Touch Memory technology and have no additional verification systems. More sophisticated bar codes use other methods of identification or authentication that cannot be cloned easily.

creates a book chapter titled: How to use Flipper Zero to prank, hack, and have fun with digital devices. It shows how to use Flipper Zero to do things like: Open other people's car doors with the Sub-1 GHz module, Change your neighbors' TV channels with the Infrared module, Pay less for bus tickets with the NFC module, Create fake barcodes with the Touch Memory module And much more!

3.4 HOW TO CREATE YOUR OWN CUSTOM APPLICATIONS WITH FLIPPER ZERO

Another main purpose of Flipper Zero is to allow you to create your own custom applications with Flipper Zero. With Flipper Zero, you can program your device to perform the functions you want, using the Python language or the C language. You can also use developer-provided libraries and APIs to access Flipper Zero's hardware and software features. You can also share your applications with other Flipper Zero users via the official website or other platforms.

To create your own custom applications with Flipper Zero, you need to follow these steps:

Choose the programming language you want to use between Python or C. Python is a high-level language, easy to learn and use, but less performant and optimized. C is a low-level language, harder to learn and use, but faster and more powerful. Choose the development environment you want to use from those available. You can use the IDE (Integrated Development Environment) built into your Flipper Zero, which allows you to write and run code directly on the device. You can also use an external IDE on your computer, such as Visual Studio Code, PyCharm, Arduino IDE, or others, which gives you more functionality and convenience.

Connect your Flipper Zero to your computer via a USB cable or via Bluetooth if you are using an external IDE. Set the appropriate USB mode for the type of language you use, such as Serial Port for Python or HID Keyboard for C.

Write your application code using the language of your choice. Follow the syntactic and semantic rules of the language, and use the libraries and APIs provided by the developers to access the functionality of Flipper Zero. You can also consult the official documentation or other sources for more information and examples.

Save your application code in a file with the appropriate extension for the type of language you use, such as .py for Python or .c for C. If you use the IDE built into your Flipper Zero, save the file in the FLIPPER/APPS folder on your device. If you use an external IDE on your computer, save the file in your project folder.

Run your application code to test its operation. If you are using the IDE built into your Flipper Zero, press the **OK** button to start running the code. If you use an external IDE on your computer, use the appropriate command to compile and run the code on your device.

Fix any errors or bugs that occur while running your application code. Check the error messages that appear on the LCD screen of your Flipper Zero or on your computer terminal. Identify the cause of the errors and modify the code so that they are resolved. Repeat the above steps until your application code works as you wish.

Using these steps, you can create your own custom applications with Flipper Zero. This can be useful for expressing your creativity and inventiveness, and for making the features you need or like. You can also share your applications with other Flipper Zero users via the official website or other platforms, and get feedback and suggestions.

3.5 How to interact with other Flipper Zero users via the dolphin network.

One of the most fun and original features of Flipper Zero is to allow you to interact with other Flipper Zero users via the Dolphin Network. The dolphin network is a peer-to-peer network that connects Flipper Zero devices to each other via Bluetooth. Each Flipper Zero device has a virtual dolphin living inside it, which can communicate with other dolphins through sound messages. You can use the dolphin network to exchange data, files, and applications with other Flipper Zero users, and to socialize and have fun with them.

To interact with other Flipper Zero users via the Dolphin Network, you must follow these steps:

Turn on your Flipper Zero and go to the Dolphin menu.
Select the Dolphin Network option and press the **OK** button.
Choose the Enable Bluetooth option and press the **OK** button.
Choose the Search Flippers option and press the **OK** button.
Wait for your Flipper Zero to detect Flipper Zero devices near you and show you a list on the LCD screen.
Choose the Flipper Zero device you want to interact with and press the **OK** button.
Enter PIN code 0000 to pair the devices.
Wait for your Flipper Zero to establish a connection with the other Flipper Zero device and show you the other user's dolphin name and avatar on the LCD screen.
You can exchange data, files and applications with the other user by selecting the Transfer option and pressing the **OK** button. You can choose what to transfer from the available options, such as RFID/NFC data, radio data, infrared data, Python or C applications, images, or others. You can also receive data, files and applications from the other user if he sends you something.
You can socialize and have fun with the other user by selecting the Play option and pressing the **OK** button. You can choose from different games that you can play with the other user, such as Tic-

Tac-Toe, Rock-Paper-Scissors, Hangman, or others. You can also receive challenges or game suggestions from the other user if he sends you something.

You can end the interaction with the other user by selecting the Disconnect option and pressing the **OK** button. Your Flipper Zero will disconnect from the other Flipper Zero device and return to the Dolphin menu.

Using these steps, you can interact with other Flipper Zero users through the Dolphin Network. This can be useful for getting to know other people who share your passion for Flipper Zero, and for making new friends. You can also learn new things from other users, and share your experiences and creations with them.

3.6 HOW TO ENJOY FLIPPER ZERO WITH GAMES, CHALLENGES, EASTER EGGS AND MORE

In addition to being a multifunctional handheld device for hacking, pentesting, and cybersecurity enthusiasts, Flipper Zero is also a fun and original device that offers you various ways to pass the time and entertain yourself. With Flipper Zero, you can play different games, participate in challenges, discover Easter eggs, and more. In this section, we will show you some of the fun features of Flipper Zero.

Games: Flipper Zero has a number of built-in games that you can start from the Games menu. You can choose from classic games such as Snake, Tetris, Pong and more, or original games such as Flipper Race, Flipper Invaders, Flipper Breakout and more. You can also download and install other games from the official Flipper Zero website or other reliable sources. You can control the games using the directional pad buttons and the **OK** and **BACK** buttons. You can also use the motion sensor to tilt your Flipper Zero and influence the game play. You can stop the game at any time by pressing the **BACK** button.

Challenges: Flipper Zero has a number of built-in challenges that you can start from the Challenges menu. These are tests of skill and intelligence that test your hacking and pentesting skills. You can choose from challenges of different difficulty levels, such as Crack the Code, Hack the Lock, Find the Frequency, and more. You can also download and install other challenges from the official Flipper Zero website or other reliable sources. You can control the challenges using the directional pad buttons and the **OK** and **BACK** buttons. You can stop the challenge at any time by pressing the **BACK** button.

Easter eggs: Flipper Zero has a number of hidden Easter eggs that you can discover by doing certain actions or button combinations. These are fun or curious surprises that make you smile or laugh. You can find Easter eggs anywhere in Flipper Zero's menu or applications, but we won't reveal where they are. You will have to look for them yourself, or consult online guides if you lack patience.

Other: Flipper Zero also has other fun features that you can use to entertain yourself or prank your friends. For example, you can use the Touch Memory module to create custom sounds when you touch ibutton keys. You can use the infrared module to create fake remote controls that do strange things to electronic devices. You can use the radio module to create interference or fake transmissions on IoT devices or access control systems. You can use the RFID/NFC module to create fake tags that contain funny or provocative messages.

Using these features, you can enjoy Flipper Zero with games, challenges, Easter eggs, and more. This can be useful to relax after a hacking or pentesting session, or to take a break from studying or work. You can also share the fun with other Flipper Zero users via the Dolphin Network, or with your friends via social networks.

In this chapter, we showed you how to use your Flipper Zero for practical, fun, and creative purposes. We taught you how to test the security of your digital systems, how to create your own applications with Flipper Zero, how to interact with other Flipper Zero users through the Dolphin Network, and how to have fun with Flipper Zero with games, challenges, Easter eggs, and more.

We hope you found this chapter useful and interesting, and that it made you appreciate your Flipper Zero even more. Flipper Zero is a unique and innovative device that offers you endless possibilities for exploration, learning, and fun. With Flipper Zero, you can discover and interact with the digital world around you, and create your own personalized digital world.

The third chapter comes to an end. I hope you enjoyed it and found it useful. In the next chapter, I will tell you about the future prospects of Flipper Zero, its potential and limitations, its challenges and opportunities. Don't miss it!

Flipper Zero:
the gadget that changes the world

In conclusion, we can say that Flipper Zero is a unique and innovative device that offers technology, hacking, and cybersecurity enthusiasts a versatile, powerful, and fun tool for exploring the digital world around us. Flipper Zero is not just a gadget, but a true open source platform that allows users to customize, modify and expand its functionality according to their needs and preferences. Flipper Zero is also a community, consisting of thousands of supporters, developers and contributors who share their experiences, ideas and projects on the official website, forum and social networks.

Finally, Flipper Zero is a project that has a vision: that of making hacking accessible, ethical, and playful, stimulating users' creativity, curiosity, and learning. Flipper Zero is not meant to be a tool to hack or damage others' systems, but to understand and improve them. Flipper Zero does not want to be a tool to spy on or steal others' information, but to protect its own. Flipper Zero does not want to be a tool to destroy or sabotage the digital world, but to build and enrich it.

Flipper Zero is the gadget that drives geeks crazy, but also the gadget that changes the world.

CONCLUSION

In this book, we introduced you to Flipper Zero, a unique and innovative device that allows you to interact with various types of electronic and digital equipment. We showed you how to use Flipper Zero to prank, hack, and have fun with devices that use radio signals, infrared, NFC, and Touch Memory. We also gave you some tips on how to use Flipper Zero with responsibility and respect for others.

Flipper Zero is a device that has many advantages, but also some risks. Among the advantages are:

The opportunity to learn and experiment with technology in a playful and creative way
The ability to customize and modify Flipper Zero to your liking, adding modules, accessories and features
The chance to join a community of enthusiasts and developers who share ideas, projects, and resources on Flipper Zero
Among the risks are:

The possibility of damaging, stealing, or violating the law by using Flipper Zero improperly or illegally
The possibility of being discovered, reported, or harassed by those who feel victimized or threatened by Flipper Zero
The possibility of being exposed to malware, viruses, or hackers that could infect or compromise Flipper Zero
To avoid these risks, we recommend that you use Flipper Zero for educational or entertainment purposes only, without harming or inconveniencing anyone. In addition, we recommend that you protect Flipper Zero from cyber attacks by using up-to-date and reliable software.

Flipper Zero is a device that still has many future prospects. Among them are:

The development of new modules and accessories that expand the functionality and possibilities of Flipper Zero
The integration of new technologies and protocols that make Flipper Zero compatible with more and more devices
The creation of new applications and games that exploit the potential of Flipper Zero
To follow up on these future prospects, we encourage you to stay updated on news and initiatives related to Flipper Zero. To do this, you can find more information and resources on Flipper Zero at the following sites:

- Flipper Zero's official website, where you can find technical features, user instructions, user manual and support forum for Flipper Zero
- The official Flipper Zero blog, where you can find the latest news, updates, reviews and interviews about Flipper Zero
- The official Flipper Zero YouTube channel, where you can find demonstration videos, tutorials, tricks and challenges on Flipper Zero
- The official GitHub repository of Flipper Zero, where you can find source code, firmware, libraries, and examples for programming and customizing Flipper Zero
- The official online store of Flipper Zero, where you can buy Flipper Zero and its modules and accessories

We hope you enjoyed this book and made you appreciate Flipper Zero. We wish you lots of fun with your Flipper Zero!

Printed in Great Britain
by Amazon

41522983R00040